Holidays Around the World

Celebrate
Chinese New Year

Carolyn Otto
Consultant, Haiwang Yuan

NATIONAL GEOGRAPHIC
WASHINGTON, D.C.

family

fireworks

lanterns

Millions and millions of people celebrate Chinese New Year—in China and around the world. The new year is a time to get together with friends and family. We celebrate with fireworks and lanterns.

∧ *A brightly colored lantern*

< *A graceful lion dancer displays fierce strength during a performance in Jakarta, Indonesia.*

The Chinese New Year

was traditionally celebrated for 15 days. Today, festivities often take place for about a week. Still, we remember the stories and our customs from long past.

The holiday begins on the night of the first new moon of the year, which marks the beginning of spring. A new moon is invisible from Earth. Over the next 15 days, it gets bigger and bigger until it is full.

Springtime is a time for a fresh start and new beginnings. It is a time of hope and promise.

A full moon shines down upon the Great Wall of China.

hope and promise

We travel to be
with our families.

China is a big country, with over one billion people. During the holidays, there are times when the whole country seems to be on the move! We may travel back to our homes, even if they are far away, so that we can be with our families and friends.

Other countries in Asia celebrate this holiday as Lunar New Year. Vietnam and Korea hold big celebrations.

When Asians immigrated to countries like the United States and Canada, they brought these traditions with them. Now many countries around the world have their own unique ways of celebrating the holiday.

< *Comfortably perched on his father's shoulders, a boy in Shanghai, China, takes in the wonder of a crowded marketplace.*

< Using gold leaf paint to draw the characters, an artist carefully paints a message of good fortune in Bangkok, Thailand.

Long before the festival begins,

we have things to do. We shop for presents, new clothes, and food. We clean our houses, stores, and streets so we can start fresh in the new year. We sweep away bad luck.

We decorate with lots of bright colors. The color gold is said to bring wealth, and the color red is considered especially lucky.

We use red paper to write special couplets in Chinese characters. Couplets are like poems or signs, calling out happy wishes and asking for good luck. We hang them around our doorways because that is where the new year will enter our homes.

> Red and gold decorations, lanterns, and blossoms promise to bring good business to the owners of this tea house in Shanghai, China.

We decorate with
bright colors.

We cook for our New Year's

Eve feast, when we will get together with family. Different foods have different meanings. We offer visitors oranges, dried fruits, and candy to make sure of a sweet future.

∧ In the Fiji Islands, hard-boiled eggs are dyed the lucky color red.

There is

plenty to eat.

A whole fish means we will have plenty to eat. Long noodles mean we will live long lives. Dumplings are crescent-shaped, like ancient gold nuggets. This means our family will be satisfied and happy. Even the amount of food has meaning. The more food we make, the more we will have next year.

sing

On New Year's Eve we gather together. We wear bright clothing. We talk and laugh. We sing, and we play music and games. We watch the New Year's Eve specials on TV. We eat! And we stay awake to frighten the Nián.

∧ *A boy in Malaysia offers a red envelope to the lion dancers. One dancer controls the movement of the lion's head, while the other forms the rest of the body.*

There are many stories from long ago about the Nián. Some say the Nián is a terrible monster. Others say the Nián is a symbol of winter that we chase away so spring can come. But our ancestors learned that the Nián was afraid of bright colors and loud noises.

play

eat

∧ Beneath a canopy of lanterns, a girl enjoys a sticky cotton-candy treat.

< Two girls play a clapping game as they stay up late on New Year's Eve.

> *Chinese drums*

Exactly at midnight on

New Year's Eve, we open our doors and windows. We let the old year out. We invite the new year inside.

We let the

old year out.

∧ *Lights are ablaze in the ancient city of Xi'an, China, where a huge golden bell rings out greetings for the new year.*

< *In Taiwan, people draw pictures with sparkling fireworks.*

Outside, people set off firecrackers and fireworks. We bang drums and make as much noise as we can. The Nián is afraid of the lights, colors, and loud noises. Now, the new year has begun!

快乐童年

Good wishes!

∧ Lucky red envelopes

On New Year's Day we pay respect to the oldest members of our families. We honor our ancestors. Children get presents and red envelopes with good wishes and new, crisp money inside. We wear our new clothes. Everything is new to celebrate the new year.

In the days to follow, there are many events and activities. We visit people. We eat special foods. There are pageants and parades. Dancers, acrobats, and musicians put on shows.

< *Laughing children in Inner Mongolia, China, slip and slide on an ice sculpture. The red characters at the top say: "Happy Childhood!"*

> *In Sao Paulo, Brazil, children perform a traditional dance.*

∧ A U.S. postage stamp honors
Chinese New Year.

On the 15th day, the
Lantern Festival takes place.
Now a full moon lights up
the night sky.

We watch the

parade of lights.

∧ *A fearsome lantern in the shape of an ancient Chinese warrior looms over a young boy in Nagasaki, Japan.*

< *A small child stares at a giant lantern during the Year of the Pig. Today, lanterns come in all different shapes and sizes.*

We greet the bright moon with lanterns. Some lanterns are simple, but some are shaped like animals, dragons, butterflies, birds—all sorts of beautiful things. We watch the parade of lights, or we join in, carrying lanterns of our own.

∧ *Dancers in Vancouver, British Columbia, bring colorful petals together to form a flower.*

During the Lantern Festival, we have folk and drum dances, and the lions and dragons dance, too. The dragons used to be made of paper, wood, or bamboo, but today they are sometimes made of lighter materials, such as plastic.

It takes a whole team of ten or more dancers to form the dragon. They have practiced together for months, even years, to learn the dances. The dancers hold each section high on a pole to help the dragon slither over the crowd. The dragons twist and turn as they make their way through the streets. They can be more than 100 feet long!

We dance with dragons!

A dance team carries a dragon in preparation for the parade in London, England.

bang

clang

There are more fireworks. There is more dancing. Drums bang, cymbals clang, and the firecrackers pop. It is loud!

The night is bright and spectacular. It is the last night of the Chinese New Year.

boom!

< Calm water reflects the bright lights and dazzling display as fireworks explode over downtown Guiyang, China.

We have done everything we can
to start the new year off right! We have
honored our families. We have had feasts
and fireworks, dancing and bright lights.
We have celebrated the end of winter.
Now we welcome the promise of spring.
We wish you a Happy New Year!
Gung Hay Fat Choy!

Gung Hay Fat Choy!

A dragon roars to life in San Francisco's Chinatown, long known for its elaborate Chinese New Year's parades.

MORE ABOUT CHINESE NEW YEAR

Contents

Make a Chinese Lantern

YOU WILL NEED:
construction paper
ruler
scissors
tape or stapler

1. Cut a one-inch-wide strip from the short end of the paper. This will be your handle.

2. Fold the paper in half, lengthwise. Use your ruler to draw a line one inch in from the open edge along the long side. This line marks where you will STOP cutting.

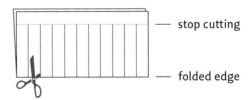

stop cutting

folded edge

3. With your scissors, cut a series of lines through the folded part of the paper toward the opposite edge. Stop at the line you've drawn. Allow at least one inch between cuts.

4. Unfold the paper and smooth it out. Then bring the short sides together and tape them. Staple the handle on top.

5. Decorate the lantern. Make as many as you like in different colors and sizes. Keep lanterns away from fire or candles.

Just the Facts

WHO CELEBRATES IT: People in China, other parts of Asia, and anywhere there are large populations of ethnic Chinese.

WHAT: A holiday to celebrate the new year and the promise of spring.

WHEN: Between January 21 and February 20, depending on the Chinese calendar.

RITUALS: Visiting family; sweeping out the old year to welcome the new; and staying up on New Year's Eve to play games, watch fireworks, and celebrate. Wearing new clothes and decorating with the color red.

FOOD: Fish, dumplings, noodles, rice pudding, New Year's cake.

The Chinese Calendar

Did you know that the whole world does not use the same calendar? Some calendars are based on the movements of the sun. Others follow the cycles of the moon. Our Western calendar is "solar," which means the days are counted by tracking the sun's location in the sky. Most countries around the world use this calendar for business and everyday purposes. But for holidays and festivals, some countries determine the date based on the moon's progress, its "lunar" phases.

Look into the clear night sky. On some nights the moon is dark. We call this the new moon. At other times, you can see anything from a crescent of light to a bright, full moon.

The traditional Chinese calendar begins with a new moon. Then the moon waxes, which means it begins to grow, becoming a full moon about 15 days later. It then begins to wane, or grow smaller, until it disappears. When the sky is completely dark, it is a new moon again. And another month begins.

In the Chinese calendar, each year has an animal symbol: Ox, Tiger, Rabbit, Dragon, Snake, Horse, Ram, Monkey, Rooster, Dog, Pig, or Rat. These animals have certain personality traits, and people born in that year are said to have those same traits.

Just for fun, look at the list at right and find the year you were born, the animal associated with it, and some traits you may have. Note: The Chinese year does not begin on January 1, as ours does. If you were born in January or February, check which day the Chinese year begins—you may actually be considered to be born the year before, according to the Chinese calendar. (For example, if you were born on January 20, 2001, you were born in the year of the dragon, 2000.)

Chinese Zodiac

OX — **1997** (February 7, 1997 – January 27, 1998)
patient, easygoing, able to achieve great things

TIGER — **1998** (January 28, 1998 – February 15, 1999)
courageous, proud, enthusiastic

RABBIT — **1999** (February 16, 1999 – February 4, 2000)
caring, imaginative, polite

DRAGON — **2000** (February 5, 2000 – January 23, 2001)
lucky, wise, powerful

SNAKE — **2001** (January 24, 2001 – February 11, 2002)
wise, elegant, musical

HORSE — **2002** (February 12, 2002 – January 31, 2003)
independent, popular, clever

RAM — **2003** (February 1, 2003 – January 21, 2004)
artistic, fashionable, sensitive

MONKEY — **2004** (January 22, 2004 – February 8, 2005)
inventive, talented, mischievous

ROOSTER — **2005** (February 9, 2005 – January 28, 2006)
stylish, adventurous, brave

DOG — **2006** (January 29, 2006 – February 17, 2007)
loyal, intelligent, honest

PIG — **2007** (February 18, 2007 – February 6, 2008)
peaceful, shy, a nature lover

RAT — **2008** (February 7, 2008 – January 25, 2009)
a strong leader, charming, hardworking

Fortune Cookies

First, you will need about 24 "fortunes." Cut pieces of plain paper into thin strips and ask your friends to write fortunes—such as "A friend brings happiness" or "A good grade is just around the corner!" Fortunes can be silly, but be sure they are positive and fun. No one wants a bad fortune! Have the fortunes ready before you make the cookies, because you need to fold the cookies as soon as they come out of the oven. You may want to wear clean cotton gloves or use a spatula to help you handle the warm cookies. You will need an adult to help you.

Fortune cookies are said to be an invention of the Japanese or of Chinese Americans. But because they contain greetings and good wishes, fortune cookies may be linked to the red couplets of China.

YOU WILL NEED:
fortunes
a mixing bowl
a measuring cup and spoons
a cookie sheet
parchment paper

INGREDIENTS:
3 large egg whites
²/₃ cup sugar
¹/₈ teaspoon salt
¹/₂ cup (1 stick) melted butter, slightly cooled
¹/₂ cup all-purpose flour
¹/₄ teaspoon vanilla

1. Preheat oven to 350°. Use a fork or whisk to blend the egg whites, sugar, and salt. Next, stir in the butter, flour, and vanilla.

2. Line a cookie sheet with parchment paper. Drop about a tablespoon of the mix onto the paper. Tilt the pan so the batter runs and makes the cookie thinner and larger—about 3-4 inches wide. Do only two cookies at a time. Leave a few inches between them so the cookies have enough room to spread out.

3. Bake for ten minutes, or until the edges of the cookies are golden brown.

4. While the cookies are still warm, turn each cookie over, place a written fortune in the center, and fold the cookie in half. Pinch the cookie closed; wrap it around a chopstick and bring the ends together. Put it in a cup or muffin tin to help it keep its shape.

Find Out More

BOOKS

Those with a star (*) are especially good for children.

*Demi. *Happy, Happy Chinese New Year!* Crown Books for Young Readers, 2003. Demi's exquisite illustrations accompany an engaging text.

*Lin, Grace. *Fortune Cookie Fortunes.* Random House, 2006. A young girl looks for the true meaning of her family's fortune cookies.

*Roberts, Cindy. *Chinese New Year for Kids.* Chinasprout, 2002. With traditional Chinese illustrations, this book is a favorite with teachers, parents, and kids.

Temple, Robert; introduction by Dr. Joseph Needham. *The Genius of China: 3,000 Years of Science, Discovery, and Invention.* Inner Traditions, 2007. This multiple award-winning, international bestseller is fascinating and includes a list of 100 things that China was the first to discover.

Yuan, Haiwang. *The Magic Lotus Lantern and Other Tales from the Han Chinese.* Libraries Unlimited, 2006. Haiwang Yuan's book is comprehensive and fun. It includes recipes, folktales, crafts, history, and facts about China. Easy to share with adults and children alike.

DRUM AND FLOWER GAME

For this game, you can use a radio or CD player, but a drum is more traditional. You also need a flower, either real or paper.

The players sit in a circle. The person with the drum sits just outside the circle. As the drum beats, players pass the flower to the person next to them. When the drum stops, whoever is holding the flower must get up, go into the center of the circle, and tell a joke or a story—or sing a song, perform a dance, or recite a poem.

When the performer is finished, the game starts over, only this time the person who just performed gets to be the drummer.

WEB SITES

Here are some fun sites full of ideas, crafts, recipes, and information:

http://www.kiddyhouse.com/CNY/
Pictures to color, games to play, things to make, and songs and poems to recite; provides links to other great sites.

http://webexhibits.org/calendars/calendar-chinese.html
All about the Chinese calendar.

kaboose.com
Great crafts for the holiday.

http://www.c-c-c.org/chineseculture/festival/newyear/newyear.html
In-depth coverage of the holiday from the Chinese Culture Center of San Francisco.

Glossary

Ancestors: All the people in our family who lived before us, such as our great-great grandparents.

Characters: Unlike our alphabet of letters, Chinese characters can be pictures of a word or a concept. They can be very beautiful.

Couplets: Couplets are like poems written in characters. During the New Year's season, couplets are usually displayed on red paper.

Fortune: Having good fortune doesn't mean having a lot of money; it means that good things will happen to you and your family.

Great Wall of China: In ancient times, Chinese people gradually built a wall across China to protect themselves from their enemies. Many parts of the wall are still in place and are favorite tourist spots.

Gung Hay Fat Choy: The expression means "Congratulations on making a big fortune!" It is the Chinese way of saying, "Happy New Year!"

Luck: Like fortune, good luck will bring your family happiness.

Prosperity: To prosper or do well. *Prosperity* often means doing well financially, having money.

Where This Book's Photos Were Taken

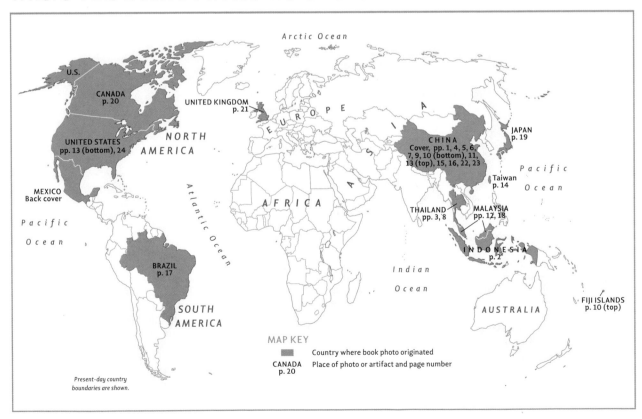

The Origins of Chinese New Year

by Haiwang Yuan

"When is the next Chinese New Year?" Few Chinese can answer this question without referring to the Chinese calendar. The calendar is lunisolar, which means it shows elements of both the lunar and solar calendars. The Chinese use the Gregorian (solar) calendar to live their daily lives, but they use the lunar calendar to celebrate their traditional festivals. Because the lunar calendar is based on the moon's revolution around the Earth, it is about 11 days shorter each year than the solar calendar. To synchronize the two calendars, the Chinese ancestors added a leap month every two or three years. Still, the calendars do not match, and thus Chinese New Year falls on a different day each year.

The Chinese lunar calendar divides a year into 24 *jiéqì* (solar terms) of 15 days each. The first term is referred to as *lìchūn,* or "the beginning of Spring." In China, the first day of the Chinese New Year is known as the Spring Festival. Because it is based on the lunar calendar, the festival is also called Lunar New Year. On the last day of this solar term, the Lantern Festival takes place. This is considered the end of the New Year season.

The Chinese have a special way of numbering the years, starting from 2600 B.C. Unlike Westerners, who see time progress in a linear way, the Chinese see it advance in repetitive cycles. Each cycle is 60 years, and each one is made up of 5 smaller 12-year cycles.

Each year within these 12-year cycles is represented by an animal in the Chinese zodiac. According to legend, the Emperor of Heaven held a race among the animals, and he assigned a year to each of the first 12 animals to arrive for the contest.

The origin of the Chinese New Year is equally mythical. It is believed that a Nián monster often preyed on humans the night before a new year. A god appeared in the form of an old man in a red cloak and frightened Nián away with the crackling of burning bamboo. Humans then learned that to survive Nián, they should decorate their houses with red colors and create loud noises with firecrackers. To the pun-loving Chinese, "survive Nián" sounds like *guònián,* or "celebrate the (new) year."

The peak of the Chinese New Year may last from three to five days, but the festive season starts about a month before. In many ways, the Chinese New Year is similar to the Christmas season. Both involve a lot of shopping, eating, gift giving, and merrymaking. Both seasons also require decorations. Instead of trees, garlands, and lights, the Chinese use paper cutouts, paintings, and couplets. Chinese children may not have Santa and his reindeer, but they do receive gifts in return for their show of respect, mostly money in red envelopes from their parents and grandparents.

Most importantly, both holidays emphasize family and friendship. The Chinese New Year is a time to reunite with family, to worship ancestors, to settle old debts, and to reconcile with those from whom you are estranged. Today, many of the old rituals and practices may have changed or disappeared, but the fundamentals persist.

Once primarily a festival of the Han Chinese, China's largest ethnic group, Chinese New Year is now celebrated by 29 of the 55 ethnic minorities in China. Beyond what is called Greater China, people in countries like Korea, Indonesia, Malaysia, Singapore, and Vietnam also celebrate the holiday. Chinese immigrants have brought Chinese New Year festivities to their adoptive countries, and celebrations are now held throughout the world.

Haiwang Yuan

Haiwang Yuan is a Professor and Web site Coordinator at Western Kentucky University Libraries. He is the author of The Magic Lotus Lantern and Other Tales from the Han Chinese *and* Princess Peacock: Tales from the Other Peoples of China.

To my aunts: Lois, Liz, Jane, and Julie

PICTURE CREDITS

Front cover, LI/Color China Photo/ SIPA; back cover: Alexandre Meneghini/ Associated Press; spine: Brand X; page 1: Guang Niu/ Getty Images; page 2: EPA/ Mast Irham/ Corbis; page 3 (top): EJ Haas/ eye ubiquitous; page 3 (bottom): Brand X; pages 4-5: Raymond Gehman/ NG Image Collection; page 6-7: Justin Guariglia; page 8: Yvan Cohen/ OnAsia; page 9: Justin Guariglia; page 10 (top): Michael Wolf/ Aurora; page 10 (bottom): Natalie Behring/ OnAsia; page 11: Kin Cheung/ Associated Press; page 12: Andy Wong/ Associated Press; page 13 (top): Karl Malakunas/ OnAsia; page 13 (bottom): Karen Zhou; page 14 (top): Shi Yali/ Shutterstock; page 14 (bottom): Udndata/ Imaginechina/ ZUMA Press; page 15: LAN/ Color China Photo/ Sipa; page 16: EPA/ STR/ Corbis; page 17 (top): Brand X; page 17 (bottom): Mauricio Lima/ AFP/ Getty Images; page 18 (top): USPS/ Associated Press; page 18 (bottom): Lai/ Associated Press; page 19: Yuki Sato/ Kyodo News/ Associated Press; page 20: Ron Watts/ Corbis; page 21: Frank Greenaway/ Dorling Kindersley; pages 22-23: Mao Chen/epa/Corbis; pages 24-25: David Dunai; page 26: Melissa Brown; page 28: Andrew Keegan

Library of Congress Cataloging-in-Publication Data
Otto, Carolyn.
Celebrate Chinese New Year / by Carolyn Otto ;
consultant, Haiwang Yuan.
    p. cm. — (Holidays around the world) Includes bibliographical references.
ISBN 978-1-4263-0381-4 (hardcover : alk. paper)
ISBN 978-1-4263-0382-1 (library binding : alk. paper)
1. Chinese New Year — Juvenile literature. 2. China — Social life and customs — Juvenile literature. I. Yuan, Haiwang. II. Title.
GT4905.O88 2009 394.261 — dc22
2008024678

Printed in the United States of America.
Series design by 3+Co. and Jim Hiscott.
The body text in the book is set in Mrs. Eaves.
The display text is Lisboa.

Front cover: Dragon dancers leap and drummers bang their drums in this joyous celebration of Chinese New Year in Beijing, China.
Back cover: A young girl hurries to join the Chinese New Year's celebrations in Mexico City, Mexico.
Title Page: A child in Beijing, China, stretches to touch a globe-shaped lantern. The round shape and the color red are said to bring good luck throughout the new year.

Founded in 1888, the National Geographic Society is one of the largest nonprofit scientific and educational organizations in the world. It reaches more than 285 million people worldwide each month through its official journal, NATIONAL GEOGRAPHIC, and its four other magazines; the National Geographic Channel; television documentaries; radio programs; films; books; videos and DVDs; maps; and interactive media. National Geographic has funded more than 8,000 scientific research projects and supports an education program combating geographic illiteracy.

For more information, please call 1-800-NGS LINE (647-5463) or write to the following address:

National Geographic Society
1145 17th Street N.W., Washington, D.C. 20036-4688 U.S.A.

Visit us online at www.nationalgeographic.com/books

For information about special discounts for bulk purchases, please contact National Geographic Books Special Sales: ngspecsales@ngs.org. For rights or permissions inquiries, please contact National Geographic Books Subsidiary Rights: ngbookrights@ngs.org

PUBLISHED BY THE NATIONAL GEOGRAPHIC SOCIETY

John M. Fahey, Jr., *President and Chief Executive Officer*
Gilbert M. Grosvenor, *Chairman of the Board*
Tim T. Kelly, *President, Global Media Group*
John Q. Griffin, *President, Publishing*
Nina D. Hoffman, *Executive Vice President; President, Book Publishing Group*

STAFF FOR THIS BOOK

Nancy Laties Feresten, *Vice President, Editor-in-Chief of Children's Books*
Bea Jackson, *Design and Illustrations Director, Children's Books*
Amy Shields, *Executive Editor, Children's Books*
Mary Beth Oelkers-Keegan, *Project Editor*
Jim Hiscott, *Art Director*
Lori Epstein, *Illustrations Editor*
Melissa Brown, *Project Designer*
Carl Mehler, *Director of Maps*
Priyanka Lamichhane, *Assistant Editor*
Rebecca Baines, *Assistant Editor*
Jennifer A. Thornton, *Managing Editor*
Grace Hill, *Associate Managing Editor*
R. Gary Colbert, *Production Director*
Lewis R. Bassford, *Production Manager*
Rachel Faulise, Nicole Elliott, *Manufacturing Managers*
Susan E. Borke, *Senior Vice President and Deputy General Counsel*

ACKNOWLEDGMENTS

For Haiwang Yuan, who seems to know everything—and who shares it graciously. For Mary Hom Quan for telling me about her family. And to Lori, Jim, and Melissa, whose artistic contributions are awesome.